Early Voyageurs

The Exciting Adventures
of the Fearless Fur Traders

by Marie Savage

To my mother, Jean Green, and my late father,
John Franklin Green, proud Canadians who
always let me paddle my own canoe.

PUBLISHED BY ALTITUDE PUBLISHING CANADA LTD.
1500 Railway Avenue, Canmore, Alberta T1W 1P6
www.altitudepublishing.com
www.amazingstories.ca
1-800-957-6888

Based on a book with the same title
by Marie Savage, first published in 2003.

Extreme care has been taken to ensure that all information presented
in this book is accurate and up to date. Neither the author
nor the publisher can be held responsible for any errors.

Publisher	Stephen Hutchings
Associate Publisher	Kara Turner
Junior Edition Series Editor	Linda Aspen-Baxter
Copy Editor	Joan Dixon
Layout	Zoe Howes

We acknowledge the financial support of the Government
of Canada through the Book Publishing Industry Development
Program (BPIDP) for our publishing activities.

Altitude GreenTree Program 🌲
Altitude Publishing will plant twice as many trees as were used
in the manufacturing of this product.

Library and Archives Canada Cataloguing in Publication Data

ISBN 10: 1-55439-710-3
ISBN 13: 978-1-55438-710-5

Amazing Stories® is a registered trademark of Altitude Publishing Canada Ltd.

Printed and bound in Canada by Friesens
2 4 6 8 9 7 5 3 1

Note to readers:

Words in **bold** are defined in the glossary at the back of the book

This book is not intended to be read as an historical study. Facts have been taken from historical records and biographies. Fictionalized details and characters were then added to the facts to create stories about the amazing lives of the early voyagers, most of whom lived in anonymity.

Contents

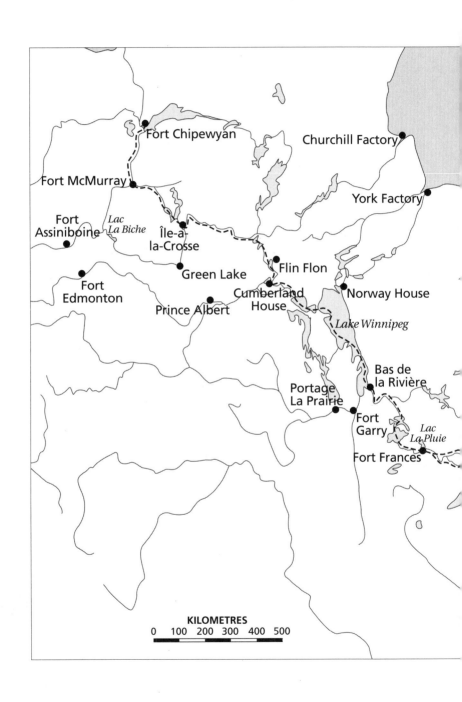

Fort Chipewyan

Churchill Factory

Fort McMurray

York Factory

Fort
Assiniboine

*Lac
La Biche*

Île-à-
la-Crosse

Green Lake

Flin Flon

Fort
Edmonton

Prince Albert

Cumberland
House

Norway House

Lake Winnipeg

Bas de
la Rivière

Portage
La Prairie

Fort
Garry

*Lac
La Pluie*

Fort Frances

KILOMETRES

0   100   200   300   400   500

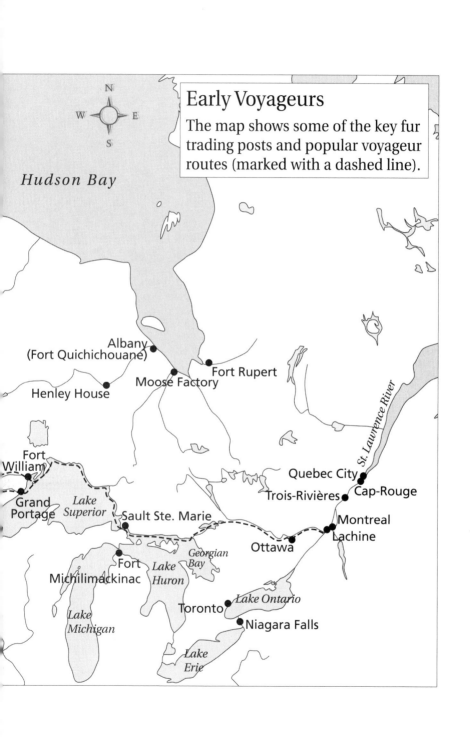

Early Voyageurs

The map shows some of the key fur trading posts and popular voyageur routes (marked with a dashed line).

Hudson Bay

Albany
(Fort Quichichouane)
Moose Factory
Fort Rupert
Henley House

St. Laurence River

Fort William
Grand Portage
Lake Superior
Sault Ste. Marie
Quebec City
Trois-Rivières
Cap-Rouge
Montreal
Lachine
Ottawa

Fort Michilimackinac
Lake Huron
Georgian Bay

Lake Michigan
Toronto
Lake Ontario
Niagara Falls

Lake Erie

Prologue

Jean-Baptiste could see the boiling waters ahead of his canoe. Their power shocked him. The steersman at the back of the canoe shouted orders to him and the other voyageurs. Jean-Baptiste pushed his paddle into the water as far as he dared. It was his first run through such large rapids. He was sure he was going to die.

Jean-Baptiste tried to swallow his fear. He focused on paddling through each dip and curve in the wild current. Wave after wave jumped the **gunnels** *of the canoe. He was sure the next one would sweep him off his perch. He gripped his paddle harder. The canoe skimmed past a boulder. The men on the left had to pull their paddles from the river to avoid it. A sharp rock bit into the birch bark at the back. Would they flip? Would the tear allow water to fill the canoe? Would they all be thrown into the river? They could drown! Only Gaston knew how to swim. He was the "***avant***," the man at the front.*

Jean-Baptiste kept paddling and praying, "Ste. Anne, keep these men safe from harm. They are good men with families. They deserve to see them again."

As suddenly as the white water had sucked them in, it spit them out. The river widened. The current calmed. They were going to make it!

Chapter 1

New France and the Beginning of the Fur Trade

Imagine setting out with only a paddle and faith in God to guide you across North America. Almost nothing was known about the continent in the 16th century. Yet men travelled its rivers and lakes in canoes. The history of these *voyageurs* is as large as their characters. It could fill several volumes. This book tells the stories of some of those brave men. They paddled the waters between Quebec and Ontario.

Jacques Cartier and the Northwest Passage
In 1534, explorer Jacques Cartier set sail from France for the New World. He sailed with two ships and 60 sailors. He wanted to find a more direct route for trade with the east. Back then, Europeans were only somewhat

interested in the fish and furs of North America. They were more interested in the east's silks and spices. They saw this continent an obstacle to go through or around.

Less than three weeks after Cartier left France, he reached Prince Edward Island. Then he sailed his ships into the Gulf of St. Lawrence. He wanted to keep sailing farther west. Every route he took led him to a bay or a dead end. He was frustrated, but he would not give up. He wanted to find the Northwest Passage. Eastern treasure awaited him.

At last, Cartier stopped in the Bay of Gaspé. He could see fishing nets and a large group of Native peoples on the shore. They were dressed strangely in pants made of skins. Outfitted in European linens and lace, Cartier rowed over. Chief Donnacona and his **Montagnais** people gave him a warm welcome. Cartier signalled the rest of his crew to come ashore.

First Contact

Cartier brought out cloth, knives, and other goods. Donnacona was pleased. Crew members were happy to accept many furs in exchange.

The two camps lived side-by-side at the shore for several weeks. Then Cartier got restless. He wanted to keep exploring westward. He went to Chief Donnacona and asked for his help. Donnacona listened carefully. He offered Cartier two of his sons, Domagaya and Taignoagny, as guides.

Domagaya and Taignoagny guided Cartier up the St. Lawrence River. Cartier was sure there was a passage west. Bad weather began to close in. With winter on its way, they could travel no farther. Cartier had to order his ships to return to France. Domagaya and Taignoagny went along.

One year later, Cartier returned. He was much better prepared. He brought along supplies for wintering in the area. He also brought more trade goods to exchange for furs. Domagaya and Taignoagny showed Cartier the way to their permanent home, Stadacona, present-day Quebec City.

Trouble in Paradise
Cartier went to talk to Chief Donnacona right away. He wanted to know which route he should take westward. Cartier did not expect Donnacona's response. The chief did not like Cartier's plan. The Montagnais had bartered the French trade goods to other tribes. They enjoyed having the only rights to these goods. Helping Cartier travel west would not help his people. Cartier sailed westward anyway. He did not know he was sailing into danger.

At Hochelaga (present-day Montreal), Cartier found 1000 Algonquins. A high palisade surrounded the settlement of longhouses. Cartier quickly learned that it was to protect the Algonquin from the Iroquois. Cartier couldn't believe that the Iroquois were as fierce as the

Algonquin claimed. He decided to stay in the area for a while. He wanted to learn more.

The people of Hochelaga were generous to Cartier and his men. They showed them how to cultivate corn and peas. They showed them how to make canoes and survive in the woods. Cartier and the Algonquin grew very comfortable together.

Cartier asked the Algonquin many questions about trade routes. He believed he could find gold and other riches farther inland. Cartier was an ambitious man. The Lachine Rapids stood in his way. So did the Iroquois. He had to find a way around both dangers.

Scurvy

Cartier and his crew of 110 men wintered at Hochelaga. They used their boats as shelter from the bitter cold. They thought they were prepared. However, they lacked fruits and vegetables. The crew became ill with scurvy. Men sank to the floor moaning and holding their heads. Sores in their mouths made eating and drinking almost impossible. Survivors wrapped their dead shipmates in sheeting. They hoped to bury them later.

Cartier finally allowed the natives of Hochelaga to help. The cure was simple to make. The brew from the bark of an evergreen tree was high in vitamin C and stopped the disease. It saved more than 70 men from a horrible death.

Cartier was glad to be rid of this problem. He was

not sure how to solve another one. His relationship with Chief Donnacona near Stadacona was not good. He was no longer concerned with the Iroquois. He was worried that the chief's people were going to turn on him. Would he be able to get home?

Kidnapped!

In May 1536, the ice melted on the St. Lawrence River. Cartier returned to Stadacona. He kidnapped Chief Donnacona, his sons, and several others. They would be insurance for safe passage out of the area. He anchored his ships not far off shore. Several canoes of Montagnais warriors paddled out to the ships. They shouted up to Cartier to let Donnacona go. Cartier refused. He would not even let Donnacona come on deck. More canoes surrounded the ships. The men and women of Stadacona refused to leave their leader. The stand-off lasted through the night.

The Montagnais filled the forest around the harbour. Their shouts got louder. At last, Cartier brought Donnacona on deck. Donnacona told his people about Cartier's plan. He would return with Cartier to meet the King of France. The King would give him great rewards to share with his people. After 10 or 12 months, he would return.

Some of the women were not convinced. It took another night to get them to return to the settlement. Then Cartier set sail for France.

Cartier was not back in 12 months or 24. In fact, it was five years before he returned. Donnacona, his sons, and their Montagnais friends had died in France. There was no happy homecoming. Nor were there the promised great riches for the Montagnais people.

The Riches of Cap-Rouge

This time, Cartier wisely stayed away from Donnacona's territory. He set up a new encampment at Cap-Rouge. (It was southwest of Quebec City.) He built a palisade around it right away. Then he explored the area. Cartier couldn't believe his eyes. Cap-Rouge was rich in gold and diamonds!

Cartier mined for both gold and diamonds. When he was satisfied, he turned his ships toward home. How glad he was to be away from New France! His commander, Sieur de Roberval, had not shown up with new supplies the year before. Men had died of scurvy and starvation. Twenty-five had died fighting the Iroquois. The survivors were more than happy to return home.

On his way back to France, Cartier stopped at the eastern end of Newfoundland. His ships floated into the harbour. They came to a stop right beside Roberval. The commander hadn't left with supplies for New France as he had promised.

Cartier was furious. Roberval ignored Cartier's complaints. Roberval ordered Cartier to return with his ships to the settlement at Cap-Rouge. Cartier argued.

Roberval refused to change his mind.

Cartier decided to ignore Roberval's orders. He and his men left under cover of darkness. Cartier felt certain he would be a hero in France. He had a cargo of gold, diamonds, and furs. When he got there, he discovered his treasure was only pyrite, or fool's gold. The diamonds were mere quartz!

Cartier never returned to New France. In the meantime, fur had become a more important trade item. More ships, and more young men, came to trade for furs. The young men became ***coureurs de bois***. They were the runners of the woods.

Mad Hatters

The Europeans put a high value on beaver pelts. The fur was perfect for hat making. The tips of the undercoat fur are slightly barbed. That made it ideal for felting. The hatters used heat and pressure on newly cleaned fur to make felt. They dyed and starched it. It was also made water-resistant. Afterwards, it was easy to shape it in any hat style.

Castor gras were dirty, greasy skins that had been slept on over the winter. They were the best. The long top hair of the beaver skins fell away with use. That exposed the downy undercoat. The less the hatters had to do to prepare the pelts, the better.

A fine beaver hat became a must in European society in the 1600s. The beaver hat was comfortable and

Various styles of beaver hat popular in the late 1700s and 1800s

stylish. The more the hat makers made, the more were demanded. Even women and children were offered styles of their own. Beaver fur became precious. None was wasted. Hairs that fell to the workshop floor were sifted from the sawdust that covered them.

There was a downside to the trade in beaver hats. Mercury was used to make the felt. The poison made hatters go mad. The term "mad as a hatter" comes from this trade.

Champlain versus the Iroquois Nation

Explorers and settlers kept coming to North America. The King of France granted monopoly charters. These charters gave fur companies the right to trade in specific areas. In return, the king expected help to settle New France with colonists.

Samuel de Champlain brought in several ship-loads of men. He was an explorer, like Cartier. He was determined to find the Northwest Passage. However, scurvy took its toll again. Champlain needed the Montagnais' help.

The Montagnais asked very little in return. However, Champlain could see what to do. He had to help them fight their enemy. He discussed plans with the chiefs. How many men did they need to frighten the Iroquois? Could they face the fiercest nation without losing?

Champlain probably thought it made sense to fight with the Montagnais against the Iroquois. But the Iroquois now considered the French their enemies.

Champlain and his friends prepared their raiding party. Gumming smoked over hot coals. They put it on the seams of the birchbark canoes so they would not leak. Dried fish was gathered for the trip. Men sharpened their knives. Champlain made sure his ammunition was dry. He was the only one on either side who carried a gun.

The day of the attack came. Champlain followed the Montagnais through the woods. They crept up on a group of Iroquois and surrounded them. The brave Iroquois stood unafraid.

Champlain raised his musket. He aimed right at the three leaders. "With the same shot, two fell to the ground." The Iroquois were surprised two men were killed so quickly. They ran.

Champlain was happy with his new alliance. He made frequent trips between New France and his homeland. On each trip, he talked to the king about the riches to be found. He also knew how important it was to colonize New France.

Étienne Brûlé

Champlain wanted to maintain good relations with his allies. He adopted a native custom. He sent young French men to live with different tribes. They learned native languages and became interpreters. Among them was 16-year-old Étienne Brûlé. He travelled to New France with Champlain in 1608. Champlain thought highly of him.

Over the years, Brûlé lived with one native group after another. He became one of the best interpreters around. He became an expert woodsman. He knew how to live off the land. He dressed like the Native peoples. He hunted and travelled as well as any of his native friends. Brûlé was probably the first European to see Lake Ontario. He travelled with the Huron to its shores. Then he explored the shores of Lake Superior. On August 1, 1615, Champlain met Brûlé on the shores of Lake Huron. Champlain and Brûlé talked about their travels. Brûlé wanted to explore the Iroquois territories. Champlain was surprised, but agreed that he could make the trip. Six months later, Brûlé was a prisoner of the Iroquois.

Captive

Brûlé plotted to get free. He spoke to the Iroquois in their own language. He made appealing promises. Brûlé knew that the Iroquois wanted part of the fur trade. Their enemies were trading old pelts for fine goods. The Iroquois could only steal goods from the *coureurs de bois* from time to time. Brûlé told them he could "bring them into agreement with the French and foes."

The Iroquois might have been interested in what Brûlé had to say. Still, they tortured and harassed him. They kept him tied up and dirty. They tried to break him down. One day, Brûlé felt they were going to kill him. The men poked at him with sticks. They jabbed him hard everywhere. They threatened to cut out his eyes. Brûlé braved it all. He could not show how afraid he really was. As soon as he did, they would kill him.

One man shouted at him. "What is that at your neck? Why do you wear this?" He was pointing to Brûlé's ***agnus dei***. Brûlé always wore the religious pendant. He believed it protected him from harm. Brûlé was alarmed. What would he do without the pendant? He looked the warrior in the eye. He yelled back at him, "If you take it from my neck, God will kill you. Everyone in your household will also die!"

The warriors laughed. This dirty beaten man was their prisoner. He was threatening them? One of them reached out and grabbed the pendant. As he did so, the skies filled with black clouds. Thunder crashed around them. The pendant was dropped.

The abuse stopped. One of the Iroquois took Brûlé into his own shelter. There, the women tended to his wounds. The tribe made Brûlé an honorary member. However, they didn't let him go right away. Finally, Brûlé was well enough to make his own escape.

He returned to Montreal in July 1618. He had been gone for 34 months. Champlain was happy to see his old friend. He wanted to put Brûlé back to work.

Champlain's goal was the same. He wanted to settle New France. But Brûlé had spent years in the woods. He was more interested in fur trade profits. Champlain heard a rumour. Brûlé may have already been working for the fur traders when he was exploring for Champlain. Champlain refused to believe the rumour.

In 1629, Quebec was conquered by agents working for the English. Samuel de Champlain left his beloved Quebec on September 14, 1629. He was taken to England as a prisoner. Brûlé refused to return to France with Champlain. Champlain had to question Brûlé's long absence from the colony. Had Brûlé helped the English? Champlain left in disgust. Soon, no one else trusted Brûlé either.

Chapter 2
The Struggle to Survive

Five years after the English threw the French out of New France, the French regained control of the colony. The two sides came to an agreement. They would return all lands and ships taken since the conflict began in 1627.

France again encouraged people to move to New France. Missionaries were eager to go. They wanted to bring religion to the natives.

Saving Souls

The missionaries sent regular reports back to their superiors in France. Their letters often showed how hard and lonely their work was. A missionary might have written the following letter:

"It has been a long day. We left the safety of the

St. Lawrence for the Richilieu River. The savages are a hardy group. They work well together. When I bow my head to pray, they point and laugh. I have come to see something in my short months here. The savages believe in nothing. I often despair of bringing them to God.

"Things would be easier here if I felt any warmth from the young men around me. The fur traders almost hiss at me as I walk past. I ask them to come to services. They refuse. They are all about business. They care nothing for their souls. Or the souls of the savages around them. I had to insist that all who come to worship arrive fully clothed. In the middle of the day, it is possible to come upon men lying in the dirt. They are stupid with drink. The young *coureurs de bois* are too used to doing as they please. They do not welcome my efforts to have them behave.

"I will travel where I must, to bring the savages to Christ. Father Robert will join me in 60 days. He will bring with him food and supplies for the long winter months. I will be glad of his company. I need him here to run the mission. I will travel yet farther up the river."

Later in his mission to the back country, the missionary may have written this:

"I have been here for some months now. I have built a small shelter at the edge of the native's settlement. This was only done after I created a proper place for worship. It stands just to the east. Several natives are now going to services each day. I am well pleased. The

A *coureurs de bois* from the late 1800s
carrying a rifle and an axe.

small trinkets needed to get their attention did not cost me much. They have proven popular. I no longer give them out at every service. I wait until the person has come for several days in a row."

The missionary might have felt he was making progress. Often his progress was only in his mind. The

Native people's lives were in the woods. They were not centred on going to religious services. Added to that, the missionaries could rarely speak the native languages.

The missionaries were frustrated with the *coureurs de bois*. They traded liquor for furs. The missionaries wanted to stop this. It led to drinking among the Native peoples. Too much drinking led to bad behaviour. Missionaries saw how careless use of liquor affected native communities. They knew the trades the *coureurs de bois* made with the natives weren't good for them.

Only a few missionaries could communicate with the Native peoples. They often turned to the *coureurs de bois* to translate for them. They also asked them to transport them to more distant tribes. Some *coureurs de bois* would not work with the clergy. The clergy were trying to change the natives' ways. What could the *coureurs de bois* gain by helping the clergy? Some Jesuits entered the fur trade to get closer to the natives. When the *coureurs de bois* realized this, it made things worse. For a time, the *coureurs de bois* and missionaries did not co-operate.

The Horror of the Pox
Epidemics swept through the native population. Whooping cough, smallpox, and measles wiped out thousands of Native peoples. They had no natural immunity to any of these diseases. The missionaries watched but could not help.

"The horror of the pox has reached my small corner of the world. The savages seem to fall to it easily. Father Robert was struck by a mild case. Other than a few small scars, his illness has been long relieved. I have been spared. My help is rejected time and again, as I approach the women. They are too sick and weak to carry their sick children any longer. They still do not want my help. For a time I could not understand why. A visiting trader finally explained it to me. The natives believe my blessings are causing the disease. Imagine believing God could harm anyone with such a horrible disease! Imagine believing that I would do such a thing! Baptisms are refused. Some families let me administer last rites. They want their family member to rest for eternity with Our Lord. It is small comfort. Many are dying without confessing their sins and accepting Christ."

By 1640, more than half the Huron nation was dead. New leaders took the place of leaders who died. New France's **governors** had to create new partnerships with the replacements.

The Company of One Hundred Associates

Profits from the fur trade were increasing. However, it was still a struggle to settle New France. Cardinal Richelieu was King Louis XIII's top minister. He saw a way to solve the problem. He wanted to link the fur trade with colonization. In 1627, the king gave the Company of One Hundred Associates control over the fur trade. There was one condition. They had to bring in 4000 settlers.

Each of the 100 associates was happy to invest the huge sum of £3000. They were a part of the fastest growing industry at the time. Europe had been trapped out. Beaver pelts were in demand but so were mink, fox, wolf, and other furs.

The charter included a full monopoly, or control, over all French lands. It would last for 15 years. This was no small deal. At the time, French lands stretched from Florida to the Arctic. They also stretched from Newfoundland and Labrador to the Great Lakes. In return, the company made a promise. They would settle New France with "natural French Catholics." They would bring in 200 to 300 persons of all occupations. This number had to be 4000 by December 1643. The Company promised to lodge, feed, and supply new settlers for three years.

Unfortunately, the company ran into problems. The *coureurs de bois* dealt with the French company only when it suited them. The rest of the time, they went farther south. They traded with the Dutch. The *coureurs de bois* did not care who was in charge. They cared only for their own survival. They had made it through illness and the threat of war with the Iroquois. They went wherever they could make the most money.

The *coureurs de bois* were happy to be independent. Still, it was a very dangerous time to be in the woods.

The trade between their enemies and the French frustrated the Iroquois. The Iroquois kept trying to cut off their trade routes. They ambushed them along the riverbanks. They attacked the fort at Ville Marie (now Montreal) over and over. Fortunately, the fort had dogs outside the palisade. They were an early warning system. Their barking alerted the settlers of possible attack.

In time, the Company of One Hundred Associates had to sub-lease their rights to all furs. The company faced bankruptcy. The colony needed the company to keep going. The settlers and the fur trade merchants got together. They agreed to form their own company. They would take on the responsibilities of the One Hundred.

A Thriving Trade

The colonists in Ville Marie and Quebec did not appreciate the rough ways of the *coureurs de bois*. The *coureurs de bois* drank a lot and partied. They lived a life of adventure. This life attracted the settlement's other young men. Many left the farm and disappeared into the woods.

The Native peoples were more eager to trade. They began to depend more and more on goods brought in from France. This gave the *coureurs de bois* more chances to make money. The governor was upset. He came up with a plan to keep young settlers on their farms.

He arranged a yearly trade fair in Montreal. It attracted hundreds of Native peoples and traders.

Colonists opened booths selling ribbons, combs, beads, and other goods. Most of the trade was finished within the first 24 hours. The **bourgeois**, or fur trade merchants, could buy large amounts of furs. In return, they gave the Native peoples brandy or watered-down rum. The drinking, dancing, and festivities went on for days.

Profit Makes Perfect

Despite the ruckus, the government encouraged the fairs. Providing a space in the colony for the traders kept settlers happy. It was better than having their strongest workers off in the woods for months. However, the *coureurs de bois* didn't want the native middlemen to share their profits. They liked to travel farther and farther inland. The *coureurs de bois* could make more money that way.

The Native peoples were just as happy to have the *coureurs de bois* bring their goods inland. It saved them many days of travel. If the natives had to travel, they went where they were offered the best value for their furs. But the *coureurs de bois* and the Montreal traders didn't want them trading with anyone else.

However, the Native peoples grew tired of this. The French traded second-rate goods. English goods were of better quality. Here, look at this kettle, the natives said to the French. It lasts much longer than the ones you traded to us. Why should we trade with you?

The fur traders of Montreal were frustrated. All

they had to offer was sent to them from France. If a shipment of bad kettles came, they were stuck with them. They had to wait until the next ship arrived. Moreover, if the *coureurs de bois* didn't bring the natives what they wanted, they wasted their travel.

The Iroquois Wars

Each season, 80 percent of the profits from the fur trade left the colony. The new company was left with only 20 percent to build up the colony. It wasn't enough. Between 1645 and 1659, the French also competed with the English trading around Hudson Bay. The profitable fur trade was changing. The traditional trading partners were changing. Epidemics had killed many. The Iroquois had massacred thousands of Huron in 1650. The trade routes became too dangerous to travel.

In 1660, rumours spread of a huge war party headed for Montreal. People could talk of nothing else. They would all be killed if 900 Iroquois attacked! One man came up with a plan. Adam Dollard, Sieur des Ormeaux, was an experienced soldier. He called for volunteers to join him. Sixteen men stepped forward. They knew they probably would not return. Most made wills. They left their possessions to their loved ones. Each of them went to church to confess. Then they headed out. The Iroquois were on their way. The men loaded their canoes. They paddled northwest for two weeks to an area called Long Sault.

There, they found an abandoned fort. It was old and in bad repair. They tried to fix the perimeter walls. However, they could see how easily anyone could breach the fort. How long would it be before the Iroquois came down the river?

Forty Huron men arrived to help Dollard and his men. Several went up river to scout for the Iroquois. Two days later, they were back. The Iroquois were almost upon them. The first of the two groups had only two canoes. Dollard and his men rejoiced. With surprise on their side, they could easily take two canoes.

The ambush was successful. Almost all the Iroquois were killed in the first moments of the fight. Dollard didn't know that one warrior got away. He had gone back to warn the other Iroquois. The next wave of Iroquois arrived. More than 40 canoes of Iroquois laid siege to the sad little fort at Long Sault. The French and Huron were greatly outnumbered.

Dollard and his men shot at their enemies over and over. The Iroquois retreated. Inside the fort, no one dared hope the small party could win. The next wave of attacks came from every direction. The men defended themselves. They were exhausted. Suddenly, most of the Iroquois vanished. Only a few stayed visible to Dollard and the Huron. They yelled threats and insults. The Huron knew more about the Iroquois ways. They knew this was just the quiet before the storm. Over the next couple of days, all but five of the Huron abandoned the French.

Dollard and his men had no food or water. They were weak and tired. The Iroquois had cut them off from the river. There could be no escape. More than 800 Iroquois had gathered nearby. Finally, they attacked in full force. Dollard and his men fought bravely, but it was hopeless. In the end, every man inside the fort died. But their sacrifice saved Montreal. The Iroquois did not attack the settlement.

Chapter 3
The Colony Survives and Thrives

Despite the danger in the woods, the *coureurs de bois* carried on. New France's governor tried to limit the number of licenses. He wanted to stop illegal trading. The *coureurs de bois* laughed at him. They kept doing business in the south.

Rumours of new beaver fields reached the colony. Several men thought they should explore the west and north. Two brothers-in-law, Médard Chouart des Groseilliers and Pierre-Esprit Radisson, went to the governor. Would he allow them to search for new areas? All they needed was a trading licence. They would provide their own expenses and supplies. They were sure of success.

A Daring Venture

The governor said no. Groseilliers and Radisson refused to give up. It wasn't their nature. The Iroquois had captured Radisson at age 16. They kept him for more than two years before he escaped. Radisson knew the Iroquois language, habits, and trade routes. Groseilliers was an experienced explorer. If anyone could make it safely through the woods, it would be these two men. They ignored the governor's decision. They prepared to head deep into native territory.

The Iroquois Are Everywhere

Groseilliers and Radisson hired other *coureurs de bois*. These men helped them paddle their goods into the north. Everyone knew it was risky. At the time, the Iroquois were ready to ambush anyone who dared to travel. For fear the Iroquois might hear them, the men hardly dared breathe. Where they found any sign of Iroquois, they did not light a fire. They slept in the canoes. They spoke only in soft grunts.

Some weeks into their journey, a man appeared out of the woods. The man held a hatchet in his hand.

"Come here! Come here!" he yelled.

The other men approached him with caution. Who was this crazy man? Was it a trick? His face was pale. He was filthy. How much of a threat could he be? However, what he said scared them all.

"Brothers, this is a good day. I am here to tell you

before I die that you cannot escape your enemies. They are spread up and down everywhere. They watch your every movement. They know you are wont to destroy them. Take courage, dear brothers. Sleep not. The enemy is at hand. They wait for you. They are so near that they see you and hear you. They are sure you are their prey."

The paddlers believed in omens. This man was a walking, talking omen. Then one of the group laughed aloud. He called the strange man a "dog."

The others took up the cry. "You're nothing but afraid yourself," they said.

"You cluck like a hen," another added.

Soon his crazed warnings brought only more jokes. Yet, as night fell, each man began to worry. What if the lunatic was right? Would they hear the Iroquois coming?

Radisson and Groseilliers were worried, too. Men did not simply appear like that. Where had he come from? Another group of *coureurs de bois* had left before them. They were in six or seven canoes. Could this poor wretch be from that group? They asked him questions. All he did was rave.

The night passed with no trouble. They made good time the next day and the one after that. Each man was tense with worry. The Iroquois might be around the next river bend. At last, they caught up to the group that had gone ahead.

They found only bodies and broken paddles. A massacre. They buried the dead. They had to get away from the Iroquois threat. They decided to move on swiftly. Paddlers worked twice as hard that day.

The rest of the trip was peaceful. In time, they found several groups of Native peoples willing to trade. They had high quality thick furs. The *coureurs de bois* wanted to visit the land where they could find these riches. Would their friends show them the way to the north? Groseilliers and Radisson traded generously. At last, they convinced the middlemen to guide them the next year. That night, it was rum for everyone!

The furs were from the north. Winters were longer and colder there. The beaver's fur grew thicker. It would be more valuable than other furs brought to France. The *coureurs de bois* spent several weeks gathering more. They had to build more canoes to transport them back to the colony.

Groseilliers and Radisson Snub the French Court

With a flotilla of 60 canoes, Groseilliers and Radisson returned to Quebec. They had packed them to the gunnels with prime beaver pelts. In addition, they brought the promise of greater riches farther north. This had to please the governor.

They were wrong. The governor had worked hard to convince young men to stay on the colony's farms. All his efforts were ruined the day Groseilliers and Radisson returned. Who could resist the exciting arrival of 60 canoes? Who didn't want to be a hero or a rich man?

The governor was furious. The men had snuck off into the north without his permission.

He didn't let their party last long. He seized the £200,000 worth of furs. He allowed Groseilliers and Radisson only enough furs to cover their expenses and their trouble. He sent the rest to France to settle the colony's debts. The furs saved the colony from going bankrupt.

Groseilliers and Radisson tried to convince the governor that there were more riches waiting in the new beaver meadows. The governor would not listen. There could be no future trips to the north. Groseilliers and Radisson had two choices. They had to live in the colony or leave. They left.

They went to the France. They got the same treatment there. Groseilliers and Radisson then decided to approach the British. They agreed to work for them. They helped them gain control of Hudson Bay.

Pioneer Colony

In 1663, the population of New France was 2500. The immigrants had adapted well to their new home. The Native peoples taught the colonists how to grow corn, peas, and squash. They enjoyed a wide variety of meat and fish. The colony had shops and an active government. It was determined to keep "good order."

The French had spent years making the Native peoples depend on their goods. They now found themselves in a strange position. They had to help support the Native peoples sometimes. When the winters were mild, beaver pelts were thinner. Thinner pelts meant lower payment. The natives couldn't trade for much. But the French needed them and their business.

Events back in France affected New France. France was at war. During the chaos, the English set up more trading posts in the north. The competition put more stress on the Montreal fur traders. Many companies had been granted control of the fur trade. The newest of these companies heavily taxed every fur brought through its warehouses. Smuggling increased to avoid the tax.

Jean Talon

In 1665, New France became a province of France. King Louis XIV appointed Jean Talon its first **Intendant**. Talon was to help govern New France. First, he wanted to get rid of the fur trade monopoly. He thought open trade might make the colony more prosperous. It might encourage all *coureurs de bois* to bring their furs to Montreal. The king rejected his ideas.

Instead, Talon decided to focus on settlement. He ordered the first official census of New France. The count was 3215 colonists. There were another 1000 soldiers and a small number of missionaries and nuns. There were very few young people. Talon wanted to change that. He encouraged the arrival of *les filles du roi.*

Les Filles du Roi

Some people needed to be convinced to move to New France. Between 1663 and 1673, Louis XIV offered a 50-livre dowry to any woman who went. The king's messengers searched the French countryside. They looked for healthy, attractive women to send to New France. They needed women who were used to hard work. More than 750 women made the trip.

Most were poor women. Some were orphans. The *filles du roi* gathered their belongings together in small bundles. They waited together on the dock for their ship to cross the Atlantic Ocean. There were set departure dates for ships. The women bunked in the hold. They had good and bad weather. Battered by the storms, many fell ill. Some refused to eat even the little they were offered. For most, land could not come soon enough.

Life in the early 1600s was very hard. The *filles du roi* were not prepared for New France. They married working men. Some men spent months away in the bush. Others worked on farms for years before they produced a decent crop. In the meantime, the women suffered.

That was of no concern to King Louis XIV. He provided the money for the plan. For the most part, it was successful. Almost all of the women stayed, married, and had children.

The Politician

Jean Talon proposed other ways to increase the population of New France. He made peace with the Iroquois. He offered the colony's soldiers land grants. They could become farmers. A full 75 percent of the regiment took up the offer.

He imported settlers between the ages of 16 and 40. He encouraged them to marry and have families early. All boys who married at age 20 or younger received a £20 gift from the king on their wedding day. A fund was set up to encourage them to have many children. The King of France provided money. For 10 children, he gave a couple £300 per year. If they had 12 children, they received £400 per year.

New France expanded by 3000 persons in the 10 years after 1672. However, to the south, the American colonies were growing 10 times faster.

Coureurs de Bois Cannot Be Tamed

In 1673, the government of New France tried again to reduce the number of *coureurs de bois.* Any young man who left his home for more than 24 hours risked jail. The governor was serious. He didn't even want young men to go out into the woods from time to time. The worst punishment for the *coureurs de bois* was "pain of death."

The real *coureurs de bois* weren't afraid. They were already in the woods. Could anyone really keep track of their movements? The part-time fellows were more likely to be caught. Anyone gone for long drew suspicion. They were accused of trading with Native peoples. They could be smuggling furs to trade with the British in the south. However, the governor's order did not stop many from trying the fur trade. The strength and stamina of the *coureurs de bois* were admired.

Amnesty

In 1681, the King of France made a decision. The *coureurs de bois* were not returning to the colony to live. The governor's laws had been too harsh. The King declared an amnesty for the *coureurs de bois*. "Bring in your furs," he said. "No punishment will be levelled against you."

Due to the amnesty, 800,000 pounds (360,000 kg) of beaver pelts came in. The market was suddenly flooded. At the time, France could absorb 50,000 pounds of furs in any one year. The king then said he would issue only 25 fur trading licenses in the colony. Each was valid for a single canoe. The *coureurs de bois* and fur traders were outraged. Smuggling began again. The licensing plan had to be abandoned.

Illegal Trade

Inland, the *coureurs de bois* kept trading posts along the northern shores of the Great Lakes. They used the Sault Ste. Marie and Michilimackinac depots. They were well away from the interference of government. The *coureurs de bois* could make their way south to the trading posts of the Dutch and the English where prices and trade goods were better. The government of New France considered them deserters. By 1683, the governor was more frustrated by illegal trade among the *coureurs de bois*.

The *coureurs de bois* knew how to survive in the wild. They were expert canoe men. They were also risk takers. Although the *coureurs de bois* had caused problems, they benefited the French, too. They secured excellent trade routes to both the west and south. The French decided they wanted Hudson Bay as well. The governor sent out a team of 100 men, including 30 soldiers. They were to capture the English forts around Hudson Bay.

It took months to reach the forts. Nevertheless, the English didn't expect an ambush. The first fort, Moose Factory, fell quickly.

In the bay was a French ship. The English had seized it earlier. The men couldn't believe their luck. They reclaimed it and re-named it the Sainte-Anne. They made it the base for their ongoing raids. Canoes scouted the next target. There was not much to report. The defences at most trading posts were minimal.

The French attacked Fort Rupert at night. The men inside fought for a short time. Then they gave up. They knew no one could come to their aid. The fort fell to the French.

Pierre de Troyes was the leader of the group. He planned to sail on to the next fort. He was sure Fort Quichichouane (Albany) would fall as quickly as the others. He was wrong. There, the English told him, "We will not surrender."

Troyes' supplies were running low. The wind had not blown in days. The Sainte-Anne and the men were in danger. Troyes gathered everyone on the ship's deck. He asked them to bow their heads to their **patron saint**. "May Sainte-Anne hear our prayers and allow us our rightful victory over the English."

The wind picked up. The Sainte-Anne and her mighty guns sailed closer to the shore. When the ship was directly across from the fort, the English surrendered.

Life in the Colony Settles Down

In 1713, England and France signed another peace treaty. The Treaty of Utrecht recognized England's claim to Hudson Bay. The French returned the captured posts. The question of the northern trade around Hudson Bay was settled.

Life in New France carried on. More immigrants filled the ships travelling up the St. Lawrence River. Their goal was to find land and farm it. At the time, only the rich could own *seigneuries*. These were long, narrow parcels of land off the St. Lawrence River. However, *habitants* could build houses to live and work on these *seigneuries*. Some were lucky to live on land already cleared. Others might have to struggle to remove the trees. It might take 7 to 10 years to completely clear a field. They left the stumps to decay. The *habitants* planted crops between the stumps. It was not an easy life.

The *habitants* had to give 10 percent of the income from their crops each year to the *seigneur*. They kept the rest. They had fishing and hunting rights on the land. From time to time, the *habitants* were asked to donate a few days of work to their *seigneur*. On these days, they improved the *seigneur's* own holdings. They also helped with roads and bridges. Still, the *habitants* lived well.

The colony flourished because of the fur trade. Furs came down to the Montreal warehouses at the end of the summer. In winter, they were sorted, cleaned, and repacked for shipment to France.

As spring rolled in, *the coureurs de bois* prepared their canoes. The traders hired crews. They purchased and stored supplies. In April or early May, the goods were readied in the Montreal warehouses. Ox carts or sleighs rolled them down to Lachine. They stayed in temporary shelters to wait for the spring thaw.

The melting away of the river ice always meant good news. The trade goods ships from France could arrive soon.

In 1758, soldiers had to meet the shipments. The English had blockaded the St. Lawrence River. This led to shortages and high prices within the colony. Colonists were desperate for whatever they could get from the ships.

Instead of goods, some of the ships carried troops.

With the troops came disease. Adding to this, crop failure meant colonists were starving. The people of New France were weak and dying. Then, the situation got worse.

The British Invade Quebec City

In June 1759, the British laid siege to Quebec City. Major-General James Wolfe led the British forces. Defending the city for France was Lieutenant-General Louis-Joseph de Montcalm. He was determined to save Quebec City from the British. The French colonists could see the British waiting below the cliffs for their chance to attack. Young boys and old men vowed to fight them off.

For months, the British fired cannons on the city. Parts of the city were left in ruins. Montcalm would not surrender. He was waiting for autumn. Dangerous winter ice packs always formed on the St. Lawrence River. To keep their ships safe, the British would have to retreat.

Wolfe knew he had to attack before winter set in. He sent some ships east. He sent some west. He was amused watching the French try to defend both positions. However, he needed a quick victory. He sent scouts to find a landing spot. It had to be large enough for all the English troops waiting to attack Quebec.

Wolfe's men left under cover of darkness. The French had sentry posts all along the river. The scouts had to stay out of sight. They travelled miles down the river from the city. They found a small area of the cliffs that sloped slightly. They landed their small craft and crept along the shore. They reached the spot they thought would be best for climbing. Sentries might be just above them. There was no way to know.

The men scrambled up the cliff. The path was good. The ground was solid. The footholds were excellent. Could thousands of men cover this ground without the cliff giving way? Would they be attacked from above? Uneasy, the scouts moved on.

At the top of the cliff, they found very few French sentries. The English scouts left without being noticed. They made their report to Wolfe. The attack began early on September 13, 1759. Wolfe and his men made their way up the cliffs. The first men to march over the edge took care of the sentries. Native peoples loyal to the French tried to fight back. Wolfe lost only a few men. The rest gathered on the open fields known as the Plains of Abraham. Then they marched on Quebec City.

Montcalm woke to bad news. The enemy was on his doorstep. He gathered his men together, but made a fatal error. He opened the gates of the city. He met Wolfe's forces on the Plains of Abraham. Neither Montcalm nor Wolfe survived the battle. Quebec City fell to the British.

Competition Heats Up

Thus, New France became a British colony in 1763. The Hudson's Bay Company expected to control "all the sea and lands about Hudson Bay and all the rivers that run into it." Yet the *coureurs de bois* were still in those woods doing business. The French fur traders in Montreal were still eager for their furs. With the British in charge, other traders moved from the south to compete for those furs. Competition meant better pay for the *coureurs de bois*. Traders who travelled inland found the Native peoples held out for the best possible price.

In 1768, the Factor (commander) at one Hudson's Bay Company trading post complained. The *coureurs de bois* were trading far into the interior. The natives had no reason to come to York Factory to trade. At first, no one listened. In time, it became plain that his concerns were well founded. "Natives build their canoes not far from the residence of the traders. They find they can get tobacco and other necessities. Being in liquor, every reason to visit the Company's Factories is forgot. The prime furs are picked out and traded."

The struggle for control of the fur trade went on for years. Finally, in 1783, the fur traders realized something. It cost too much to work independently. To compete with the Hudson's Bay Company, they joined forces as the North West Company. They had a great advantage. The Hudson's Bay Company men still had to wait for decisions made in England. The partners of the North West Company could make decisions on the spot. They hired a huge number of *coureurs de bois* to transport goods inland and furs back to Montreal.

Chapter 4
The Voyageurs

For a long time, the *coureurs de bois* had worked as independents. They worked for one trader or another, in canoe brigades. Now, they all worked for the North West Company. Together, they became known as the voyageurs.

The voyageurs used canoes to transport goods. The brigade's "guide" was the leader of the group and responsible for the canoes. If water leaked into the birchbark canoe, the goods could get soaked. Then the canoe would be pulled even lower in the water. Canoes already sat low in the water, just inches from their gunnels. They were sealed at every join with "gumming." This was a mixture of animal fat, tree sap, and charcoal. The guide checked each 36-foot (11-metre) canoe carefully before leaving.

The Right Man for the Job

In the meantime, the *bourgeois,* or fur trader, put out the call for voyageurs. It didn't take long to find men willing to power the canoes. They came to the bourgeois' offices.

"My name is Philippe. I am ready to work," a young man might say.

The bourgeois would look up from his desk. He would look for certain traits in the young man. He needed strong men shorter than 5 feet 4 inches. They had to fit on top of the cargo in the canoe. Men with long legs often quit. The bourgeois knew good men ran in families. "Do you have a brother?" he might have asked Philippe. Many of the crews were hired in this manner. One man told another about the chance. Travelling together into the back country would be an adventure!

The men often had to paddle 16 hours a day for weeks. They had to **portage**, or carry the canoes where they couldn't paddle them. They had to run over the narrow, rough portage trails quickly without tripping. Short, strong men could do this. Their centre of gravity is close to the ground. Voyageurs developed large arms and massive back muscles. They became even stronger from their work.

The Fine Print

When the bourgeois chose Philippe as a voyageur, he presented him with a contract. Most voyageurs could not read or write. Many signed their contracts simply with an X. The contract hired a voyageur for one to three years. Like all voyageurs, Philippe agreed not to desert or give aid to a rival company. If he did, his fellow voyageurs would be hard on him. The voyageurs were a tightly knit group. They had to be. It was their only chance for survival.

When he signed on, Philippe was given one-third of his wages. The bourgeois' staff also helped Philippe put together a kit. The North West Company dressed and fed its workers. He received a wool blanket, shirt, pants, and two handkerchiefs. He also got several pounds of twist tobacco.

The Canôts du Maître

It was time to leave. The guides had approved the canoes for travel. The men brought the trade goods out of the sheds at Lachine. They loaded them into the huge **canôts du maître**. Each Montreal canoe carried four tons of cargo. The cargo was made up of two-thirds trade goods and one-third supplies. One surviving record listed the items in a single canoe:

	Each	Total
16 bales containing each 1 pc. stroud (cloth) & other dry goods	100	1600 lbs.
12 kegs rum, ea. 8 gals.	80	960
2 kegs wine, ea. 8 gals.	80	160
4 kegs pork and beef	70	280

	Each	Total
2 kegs grease, 1/3 tallow, 2/3 lard	70	140
1 keg butter		70
3 cases iron work	100	300
1 case guns		90
6 kegs powder	80	480
4 bags shot and ball	85	340
4 bags flour	100	400
4 rolls Brazilian tobacco	90	360
4 bales tobacco	90	360
63 packages	TOTAL	5540 lbs.

In addition:		
9 men	140	1260
9 bags	30	270
1 keg rum		80
6 bags bread or pease	100	600
4 kegs beef or pork	70	280
1 travelling case		80
Kettles, poles, paddles, oil-cloth, gum, bark, etc.		140
	TOTAL	8250 lbs.

Each voyageur had his own "bag" for personal things. He might bring a shirt or two and an extra pair of moccasins. Some brought trinkets to trade along the way. Voyageurs could each bring up to 40 pounds (18 kg).

The bourgeois put at least one keg of rum in each canoe. They liked to reward their voyageurs with a "cup of grog" after a very long day or difficult portage.

Some items were supplies the crew needed every day. Kettles were black tin pots or brass cauldrons. Cooks made the evening meal in them. Several poles lined the bottom of the canoe. Voyageurs used them to move through shallow waterways. The poles also kept the trade goods out of any water that seeped in. Oilcloth acted like a tarp. Gum and bark were brought for repairs. There was no time to locate and strip trees along the way.

The Big Adventure

The voyageurs said long goodbyes to their loved ones. Then they hopped into their assigned canoes. Would they see their families again? Dangers filled every trip. A slip during a portage or a tipped canoe could end a voyageur's life. An ambush by bandits was also possible.

The voyageurs pushed off to begin the 2000-kilometre run. They went from Lachine up the Ottawa and Mattawa Rivers. They crossed Lake Nipissing. They went down the French River to Georgian Bay. Then they paddled on to Fort William on the northwest shore of Lake Superior.

Crowds of people lined the shore to see the voyageurs off. Philippe would have heard their cheers as he readied his paddle. The red-ended paddles sliced through the water at 45 strokes per minute. Then they moved faster to a steady pace of 55 strokes per minute. At the bow of the canoe, the company flag fluttered in the wind.

The voyageurs shouted back and forth between the brigade canoes. Each crew tried to outdo the other. The eight canoes leapt through the water. The bourgeois sat in the middle of Philippe's canoe. His hands never touched a paddle.

An hour later, the ***gouvernail*** called for a break from the back of the canoe. Paddling stopped at once. The voyageurs opened their beaded tobacco pouches. A ***sac-à-feu*** hung from a brightly coloured woven sash at their waists. The sashes were called ***ceintures fléchées***.

Life on the River

The voyageurs took out enough tobacco for a quick smoke. They lit their clay pipes and rested. "Pipes away," the *gouvernail* called. *"Allez!"* They were off again. On a good day, the voyageurs could paddle their canoe six to eight kilometres an hour.

It was near the end of the second leg of the trip out of Montreal. The *gouvernail* would soon call another break. The voyageurs planned to go ashore at Ste-Anne-du-Bout-de-L'ile (Ste. Anne at the end of the island). There, they could honour their patron saint.

First, they had a job to do. The voyageurs had to get their canoes past the rough waters ahead. Philippe helped portage some of the goods around the point. At the same time, the *gouvernail* and a few men stayed aboard. They paddled the canoe to the meeting spot on the other side. They watched for their man on shore to guide them in. Then the canoe was reloaded. The voyageurs were glad of these **demichargés**. Moving half the cargo was easier than moving all of it. The bourgeois had only himself to worry about. It was not his job to help with the cargo. He was a passenger along for the ride.

Their cargo was safely moved. Then Philippe and the other voyageurs walked up to the chapel. They offered a prayer to Ste. Anne for their companions and for their safe return to Montreal in the autumn.

A Man's Place is in the Canoe

At the very rear of the canoe was the *gouvernail*. He was the steersman of the canoe. His long, thick-bladed paddle kept the canoe on course. In front of him was the *milieu*, or middleman. These voyageurs were usually the least experienced. This was where Philippe sat. The bowsman, known as the *avant,* sat at the front of the canoe. He kept watch for dangers lurking in the water. A submerged log could end the trip.

Birchbark was an excellent building material for the canoes. It was also easily damaged. A jagged rock or a hidden log could prove dangerous. The crew might lose more than their cargo. They might lose their lives. Most voyageurs did not know how to swim.

Men with more experience got the more important jobs. They had to "read" the rivers. They also had to keep the cargo and the men safe. From time to time, the *gouvernail* called for the canoe to be unloaded. To empty and portage each 300-pound (136-kg) canoe and its load to the next **put-in** was called a ***décharge***.

Portaging — A Necessary Evil

The voyageurs were quick to remove all the goods and provisions. They transported them to the put-in. Then they returned for more. If it was a very long portage, there might be several stops or ***posés***. The voyageurs worried about bandits. They had to move the goods in stages to prevent stealing or ambush. Everything was carried to the first *posé*. Then they moved it to the next, and so on, until they reached the end.

In some places, only a *demichargé* was needed. The *gouvernail* poled through the difficult passage with the help of one or two other voyageurs. Sometimes a branch got in their way. One of the voyageurs might jump out onto it. His weight would bend it enough to allow the canoe to pass. Sometimes the *milieux* would pass the canoe hand-to-hand in the water. In this way, they could bring it up over rocky inclines. At other times, a towline from shore could keep the canoe steady. The towline could also prevent it from sliding backward down the rapids. If the canoe got stuck, the voyageurs called it ***dégradé***. They probably swore, too.

So it went, day after day, on the long trip to Fort William. The hard-working voyageurs liked a good time. However, there was time only to tell a few stories after their evening meal. The voyageurs had to check their canoes for holes and patch them. Then the men rolled beneath their overturned canoes on shore. They fell asleep quickly. Their work would begin again all too soon.

A Day on the Water

"*Alerte!*" came the call to rise.

The voyageurs often started their work before the first light of dawn. First, they had to right the canoes. Then they had to pack them correctly. Cotton string held each canvas-covered bale, or **pièce**, together. This string was inspected on all sides. Back in Montreal, the guide had marked them. Each *pièce* and barrel bore the company's mark in India ink. A second mark showed its place in the canoe. In re-packing the canoe, this order was repeated. The weight had to be spread evenly.

The passengers were the last pieces of "baggage." Each one was hoisted onto a voyageur's back. They were piggybacked out to the canoe one at a time. The voyageurs did this to save the canoe. No one wanted a passenger to kick a gummed seal by accident. This could cause a leak and a delay.

Packed and ready to go, the voyageurs pushed off. No breakfast was offered. The first meal of the day came hours later. They had to make many kilometres first.

Imagine seeing a brigade speeding up the river. Each canoe carried a heavy load. Legend says the voyageurs' perfect timing made the canoes fly across the top of the water. Voyageurs weren't the first to travel in brigades. Nor were they the first to paddle the inland waters. The Native peoples had been doing it for years. In fact, many voyageurs were native or men of mixed blood.

The master builders of birchbark canoes were the Ojibwe and other Native peoples. A canoe took a lot of abuse on its everyday travels. It could rarely be used for a second season. As the fur trade grew, so did canoe making. Voyageurs required hundreds of canoes every year.

In time, the French needed more canoes than the Native peoples could make. Several colonists started canoe factories. The Le Maître family of Trois-Rivières owned the best one. Their name became the standard for all large cargo canoes.

There were several different sizes of canoes. Philippe's crew used the largest. *Le maître* canoes carried goods and furs between Montreal and Fort William. These canoes travelled well on large waterways and the Great Lakes. There were times when *Le Maître* canoes were too bulky. On northern waterways, smaller canoes of different sizes were better. Express canoes relayed urgent messages from post to post. It was an honour for a voyageur to paddle an express canoe.

The voyageurs paddled for several hours. At last, they stopped for their morning meal. Not a single foot touched dry land. Breakfast was eaten in the canoe. The men ate a bit of jerky (dried meat) or stale biscuit. They washed it down with water. They scooped it from the river with their noggin. This was a cup carved from a knot of wood. It hung from their *ceintures fléchées*. Staying on the water saved them time. It also kept them away from the bugs on shore.

The voyageurs finished the morning meal. The journey began again. The voyageurs faced at least one portage every day. There were 36 portages between Montreal and Fort William. Philippe soon learned that the voyageurs typically carried two 90-pound (40-kg) bales. The first hung down Philippe's back, wrapped with a "tumpline." This strap went around his forehead. The second bale was placed sideways on top of the first.

Voyageurs often boasted about their heavy loads. The company paid them extra for every bale they carried in addition to the first two. Rising to this challenge had its drawbacks. Hernias were a known curse to the voyageur. Records show the facts. More than one voyageur died en route from a hernia.

Most voyageurs handled their duties without mishap. They adapted to their surroundings. They used a strange dogtrot to run the goods over the portage trails. Up, down, over roots and rocks, and between hills, the voyageur trotted through the wilds.

Day's End

Evening camp often followed a very long portage. Enough open space had to be found for cargo, canoes, and men. Cooks rushed to find enough firewood. They had to start fires to cook the evening meal. They would half-fill their kettles with fresh water and set them to boil. From their stock, they added dried peas or corn. This made a thick mush when cooked. Salted pork and some lard went into the mush.

Sometimes, local Native peoples offered fish or duck to Philippe and his fellow travellers. The natives traded fresh food for rum or brandy. From time to time, the voyageurs found other things to eat. They enjoyed fresh berries. At some camps, picking berries was as easy as reaching into the nearest bush. They sometimes found honey or turtles nearby. The cook gladly added these to the nightly mix. Mush and pork was the voyageurs' standard evening meal. This daily diet of pork earned Philippe and his buddies the nickname, ***mangeurs du lard***.

Why was the voyageur diet so limited? The woods were teaming with animals. The rivers were full of fish. The voyageurs didn't have time to hunt. They had much to do once they camped for the night. The canoes were strong. However, the gumming was brittle. It broke off regularly. The cargo had to be checked to ensure the goods did not become wet.

After their evening meal, Philippe and the men settled around the campfire. There was a short time for conversation and telling stories. The men were good company for each other. Philippe laid down each night to the calming sound of running waters. Small smudges lit through the night kept the bugs away. Not all of them were unwelcome. Philippe might have gone to sleep watching fireflies.

No Two Journeys the Same

Each day brought new challenges for the voyageurs. Routes changed from season to season. Beaver meadows could keep an area flooded one year. They might be gone the next. The men then had to find new **take-outs** and put-ins.

Rapids might be easy to run one season. They might rip out bottoms of canoes the next. Voyageurs were scared out of their wits by the crazy water on some of the runs. The men pulled as hard as they could. They had to, even when waves threatened to toss them off. The canoes surged forward through the roaring water. Boulders could look small from a distance. Close up, they could be very large. If a man hit one, he could break his neck.

"Pull!" yelled the *gouvernail*. He knew what the new men did when they saw the size of the waves licking over the bow. They pulled in to protect themselves. This action could capsize the canoe. "Pull!" he yelled again.

Where possible, they used sails. This was tricky. It was tempting to sail straight across Lake Nipissing.

However, the results could be disastrous. High winds created swells big enough to swamp canoes. The canoes had large, upswept bows. This made them more stable in high waters. However, the danger of capsizing was real. Sometimes, several canoes were lashed together. This made a more stable sailing vessel. On occasion, high winds and heavy rains blew in on the brigade during a crossing. Then the guide called for a stop on the opposite shore. The voyageurs had to rest. They had to check the goods again.

The mouth of the French River was famous. It had to be poled. This final stretch of white water was long and tiring. It was also dangerous. Some of the goods and provisions had to be unloaded. The voyageurs had to lighten the canoes. Then they could ride higher in the water. Portaging here was never easy. Exposed roots and sharp stones made the going tough. Pathways were little more than thin trails through the bush. Some went right out over the river.

Some men took on the task of portaging the goods. Others stayed in the canoe to aid the *gouvernail* as he poled ahead. Those who stayed held the ropes tied to either end of the canoe. They trudged along the shore trying to match the *gouvernail's* pace. These towlines kept the craft from being swept away. It was slow, hard work.

The voyageurs were thrilled to finally get through the area. They often tossed their **perches** away. They wouldn't need the poles again until the return trip.

Dangerous Journey

The voyageurs treated white water with great respect. To travel carelessly meant losing men and cargo. Worse, it might mean losing one's paddle. The experienced ones warned Philippe not to lose his paddle. Without it, a voyageur was useless. There were no extra paddles carried in the canoes. It was impossible to carve one overnight. Losing a paddle meant losing face. Who wanted to be like the useless passengers? They were just along for the ride.

Every so often, Philippe and his crew might spy a broken paddle. It was usually bound in the shape of a cross. These marked the places along the way where other young men had died. As they passed, Philippe and his friends bowed their heads. They said a short prayer.

Voyageurs transported masses of trade goods and people. Records show they did not lose many voyageurs, passengers, or cargo. Still, accidents did happen. Voyageurs got hurt along the way. They broke bones. They gashed their arms and legs. They got upset stomachs and other ailments, too. Most often, their ailments were treated with a shot of rum and a pat on the back.

The Danger of the Falls!

The closer the brigade got to Fort William, the longer the days. The brigades reached Five Mile Rapids. That meant they were only a few hours away from Recollet Falls. It was a long 29 kilometres of flat water approaching the falls. During that time, the other voyageurs could tell Philippe about the take-out above the falls. It was only three metres from the edge of the falls. A mistake there could cost lives.

They drew closer to the falls. The *gouvernail* placed the canoe into a current that brought them closest to shore.

"*A droit! A droit!*" (To the right!) he yelled above the roar of the falls.

The current was strong. It threatened to sweep them over the edge. Voyageurs on the right pulled hard. Voyageurs on the left back-paddled with the *gouvernail*. The canoe swung in to shore. The voyageurs leapt out to draw the towlines tight. Afterward, the portage around the falls wasn't nearly as exciting.

Within a few days, most of the trip was behind them. Philippe and the other voyageurs cheered at the sight of Lake Superior. They stayed close to shore for safety. The voyageurs sang their favourite songs.

By the clear running fountain
I strayed one summer day,
The water looked so cooling
I bathed without delay
Many years have I loved you
Ever in my heart you'll stay

Love and longing were the usual themes of songs. Voyageurs were away from their families for months at a time. Singing helped keep their spirits up. Voyageurs with good voices who knew many songs were often paid extra.

"*Souffle, souffle, la vieille,*" the voyageurs called. "Blow, blow, old woman." Tobacco was tossed onto the waters as an offering to *La Vieille*, the wind.

Even without a wind, the canoes travelled quickly. At the end of the day, they measured how far they had come. They counted the number of pipes they had smoked. Each pipe represented about seven or eight kilometres' travel.

Hard Decisions

The dangerous waters of the inland rivers were behind them. However, travel on Lake Superior also had its risks. Crossing open stretches of water to save time was dangerous. The canoes risked the high winds. A guide had to study the weather carefully. He had to be sure before he directed his brigade to try a crossing between two points of land. Sticking to the shoreline was always safer.

Cheers greeted the sight of the Sleeping Giant. It was a landmark island in Lake Superior. Fort William was only days away. Soon, the voyageurs would see their families. Philippe looked forward to the chance to have some fun at the expense of the **hivernants**. These were the men who wintered in the northwest. They travelled to Fort William laden with furs.

Chapter 5
Life in the Company

N orth America was large. But that did not mean that the *coureurs de bois* could travel wherever they wished. The *coureurs de bois* respected the Native peoples' ways. The natives held claims to the rivers and lakes. Trade routes had been a part of different families for generations. One arm of a river might belong to one family. The other arm might belong to another. To pass along a particular river required payment of a toll. Travelling without the owner's permission was serious. It was almost like declaring war.

There was one way for the fur traders to ensure good relations for years to come. They could marry into a native family. Hundreds of *coureurs de bois* took native wives, *á la façon du pays*. This meant "in the way of the country." In other words, they married without clergy or church. Instead, they married according to native custom.

The Marriage Ceremony

In native marriage ceremonies, a man offered his loyalty to his wife. He also pledged his loyalty to her family and her tribe. On the day of the wedding, the groom might prepare a speech. It would compliment his new father-in-law. He would also look through his belongings and trade goods. What was the best item he had? A fine gun or a thick blanket would honour the family. If the father-of-the-bride accepted the gift, the man could marry his chosen. Then the man and his father-in-law would smoke a *calumet* (peace pipe). The bride might have watched the gift presentation. Otherwise, she probably did not take part in the ceremony.

Women of the Fort

The voyageurs needed wives who understood their way of life. Better yet, they needed partners who could help them. Native women knew how to build canoes. Women made moccasins and snowshoes. Women also knew how to find edible roots and prepare soothing salves.

Many women married voyageurs who visited them only in the summer. However, the country wives were always addressed by their married name. They were also known as "the women of the fort." Many lived in or near a trading fort with their children. They might share a building with several other families.

The country wives guided, and interpreted for, visitors to the fort. They also helped with the spring planting and autumn harvest. Their skill at net making was useful. They caught whitefish in their nets. Then they salted it for the warehouses. Sometimes, this salted fish was the only winter food besides potatoes.

Their skill at gathering wild rice was also praised. The women gently bent the long rice plant stalks over the gunnels. Then they beat them with a stick. This dislodged the rice onto the canvas lining the bottom of the canoe. In a week, they could fill several canoes with the tough grain. They packaged the rice for trade or storage. They could do what they wished with it.

The country marriages could be good for the bourgeois, too. The voyageurs had to ask their permission to marry. Sometimes, he charged them for the privilege. He could have a few days' extra work from every man who wanted a country wife.

Some men worked at the fort year-round. These "freemen" took care of the winter needs of the fort. They cared for the animals and kept the buildings in good order. They also helped in the warehouses and with other chores. In the spring, they pulled ice from the river for the icehouse.

The freemen had been voyageurs. Their contracts had expired. The company released them. Most voyageurs retired before they reached their 40th birthday.

For women married to freemen, life was very good.

The women of the fort were considered an asset for many years. Naturally, the missionaries in New France did not approve of the marriages *á la façon du pays*. However, they could do little with the voyageurs.

European Women Set a New Standard

Clerks were under different pressure. Their wives had to suit their positions in the company. Men who wanted to move up in the company had no choice. They could not marry native women. Their wives had to be European women. They had to be born and raised in the upper class of society.

In later years, more European women immigrated to Upper and Lower Canada. These women had no skills to offer their husbands when it came to living in the wilds of Canada. Yet they criticized the customs and abilities of the country wives. To them, it was more important to be a "lady." Mixed-blood girls could study at top schools in Upper and Lower Canada. Yet they were often left out socially. European women expected to hire mixed-blood women as servants. They did not expect to sit across from them at dinner parties.

The Hivernants

The *hivernants* (winterers) were voyageurs who earned the right to call themselves **hommes du nord**. These men of the north lived in the bush all year round. Some

spent years up north, in the ***pays d'en haut***. They made
it to Fort William each year. Like the voyageurs, *hivernants* could be Scottish, native, or French Canadian.

One young Scot named Stewart remembered hear-
ing stories of these wild men before his first season
as one. These men had lived through the hardships of
winter and survived to tell about it. No one could claim
the name of *hivernants* on their own. They first had to
submit to a ritual "baptism."

Leaving Fort William at the end of the season,
Stewart didn't know what to expect. The *hivernants*
stopped at the first take-out. There, they tied their
canoes to trees on the shoreline. Then the *hivernants*
gathered around Stewart and other new voyageurs.
One of them cut a bough from a nearby cedar tree. He
took the bough to the water's edge. There, he dipped
it into the cold waters of Lake Superior. He carried the
sopping branch back to where the new men waited on
their knees. He raised it above their heads and sprinkled
their upturned faces with water. Stewart and the other
young men then had to repeat the *hivernant* promise.
They promised to always stop and baptise other new
men in this way. Secondly, they promised never to kiss
a voyageur's wife without his permission. The ceremony
was over. Stewart's new friends fired several rounds into
the air. They shared a welcome "cup of grog."

The *hivernants'* work was different from that of the
voyageurs. The northwestern waterways were not large

enough for the giant Montreal canoes. The *hivernants* paddled *canôts du nord.* These smaller canoes carried fewer men and goods. At designated posts, the canoes separated. Each man travelled down smaller rivers and streams. Their goal was to reach the most remote of native villages. There, they would trade what they could. They also set up their winter camp.

Stewart's only shelter was a canvas tent. He had a lot of work to do before winter set in. Stewart needed to cut a large supply of firewood. The backbreaking work took weeks. He needed a dog sled to make winter runs to more distant tribes. The local Native peoples helped him build one. They also provided the dogs to pull it.

Sled Dogs and Mutt Motels

From time to time, Stewart and the other *hivernants* travelled to the northwest trading forts. They went to renew supplies or store furs. While they were there, they bragged about the strength and endurance of their dogs. A *hivernant's* animals were important to him. The dogs had excellent care. Still, they were more wild than tame. To hold them, dog hotels sprang up outside forts. Inside the fort, the dog owners could take care of business.

The winter pace was slower. The *hivernants* had more time for fun. They were always looking for a contest. Sometimes, they raced their dog sleds against others. Stewart tied his warm *capot* closed with his *ceinturé fléchée.* Then he urged his dogs forward. They went faster and faster. The sled was always in danger of flipping over. Spills happened. Righting a sled and gathering furs from the snow banks was part of the fun.

Heading Home

The end of winter approached. The *hivernants* reversed their routes. On the way back, they rejoined their former crews. Canoes flew side-by-side across Lake Winnipeg again. The wind burned the *hivernants'* faces. Blisters formed on their hands. Kerchiefs dipped into the lake kept their necks cool.

They sang for hours as they paddled. It made them very hungry. The *hivernants* were not *mangeurs du lard*. They travelled with a supply of pemmican. Pemmican was nutritious. Stewart and his friends bought it from the Native peoples who traded in the northwest. They made it by drying meat in strips. Pound to a fine pulp, it was placed in a buffalo hide bag. The bag was called a *taureaux*. Boiling buffalo fat and 16 pounds (7 kg) of Saskatoon berries were added. The bag was sewn shut and sealed with tallow. Pemmican never spoiled.

While they paddled, the *hivernants* looked for the landmarks that marked the route to Fort William. They looked for "lobsticks." Passing voyageurs liked to lob off the uppermost branches of the tallest trees. The lobsticks could be seen from a great distance. Sometimes, it marked the passage of an important passenger. It was a way for voyageurs to honour their guests. It was also a sure-fire way to get an extra "cup of grog" from the *bourgeois* passengers.

Canôts du nord carried fewer men. Still, their work was as difficult as that of the voyageurs in the larger Montreal canoes. Portages and poling were still necessary. Sometimes they had to use a towline to bring the canoe safely through low waters. On occasion, Stewart and his buddies jumped into the cold water. They had to guide the canoe past sharp rocks and dangerous eddies.

The Voyageur's Fund — Early Insurance
The *hivernants* might survive the winter and the wild waters of the spring run-off. Still, other dangers threatened them on their journeys. Forest fires could start anywhere. Being caught in a raging fire was horrible to imagine. Bears and wolverines shared the woods. Lucky *hivernants* travelled without meeting anything more fearsome than a moose or great blue heron.

Sometimes voyageurs died while working for the company. Others suffered disabling injuries. Surprisingly, the men had insurance against such events. Both voyageur and company gave to a special Voyageur's Fund. In his contract, each voyageur pledged one percent of his earnings each year. The company made yearly grants to the fund. It helped those who could no longer work because of age or disability. Widows received a small amount from the same fund.

The *hivernants* got closer to Fort William. They joined with other canoes. Races between crews might seem fun. They were also risky. No one wanted to lose a winter's work by tipping a canoe of furs into the water. It was time to reap their rewards. Their wages were waiting for them at Fort William. So was next year's allotment of clothing, knives, and an assortment of beads.

Chapter 6
The Summer Gathering

Before they reached Fort William, the brigades slipped into a nearby shore. Everyone hopped out of the canoes to clean up. The voyageurs washed the sweat and grime from their faces. They also found clean shirts in their bags. Cook found a suitable boulder for the men to sit on it. He trimmed their hair.

When everyone was ready, the brigade paddled toward Fort William. There, noise of cannon fire welcomed them. By the end of June, brigades arrived at Fort William daily. During the boom years of the fur trade, more than 3000 men were welcomed at the fort each summer.

Teamwork
Philippe and his buddies grabbed towlines. They tied the

canoes to the huge wharf in front of the fort. Then they formed a line to hand the goods from one man to the next. In this way, they emptied the canoe and stacked the goods on the wharf. Then every man grabbed a load. The guide directed them to carry their loads to one of the warehouses inside the fort. The men laughed and boasted of their strength. They tried to outdo one another carrying the goods along the fort's pathways.

The men were ready for a few days rest. This was the highlight of the journey. They could spend days and nights at the fort. They could enjoy the company of other voyageurs.

Each voyageur also had to give the fort six days work. This was in their contracts. Philippe might have to help put up a new building. He might repair rotting boards. Often the voyageurs moved canoes in and out of the canoe shed for repair. Others weeded gardens, or gathered birch strips from the woods. Some mucked out stalls of the farm animals.

At its peak, Fort William had 42 buildings. They spread out over 125 acres. The farm had horses, sheep, cows, and oxen. There were a large number of field gardens. A 15-foot palisade enclosed the whole fort, except for the farm.

The voyageurs' camp was outside the palisade, too. Here, Philippe and the other *mangeurs du lard* stayed. They ate their meals from kettles over open fires near the wharf. They slept in hundreds of small canvas tents. Each was large enough for only a man or two. Stewart and the other *hivernants* kept their camp at the other end of the wharf. Fights often broke out between the camps.

The Company Hierarchy

The Great Hall inside the fort was a giant meeting room. It was time for business. All the company partners came from east and west. They received reports on the business of distant posts. They discussed types and value of trade goods. They decided their plan for the next year. In addition, they gave out promotions.

The partners were called the Nor'westers. They had their own pecking order. In the Great Hall, they sat according to their station within the company. The more comfortable chairs went to the partners. The clerks had to make do with whatever they were offered.

Rank also decided sleeping quarters. Montreal bourgeois slept in bedrooms at either end of the Great Hall. The Northwest House had 12 bedrooms. It housed the wintering partners. The Bell House was set up for the "superior" clerks. Apprentice clerks and interpreters shared the East House.

The clerks could hope to become partners in time. They heard tales of the Montreal partners' lifestyles and beautiful mansions. These tales helped them bear the long winters at distant forts.

If Philippe were useful as a voyageur, he could

perhaps be a translator one day. However, he would never move farther up in the company than that.

Dinner and Dancing in the Great Hall

At the top of the Bell House was the bell. It rang to signal the end of the working day. It also rang to bring people to meals. Despite the wilderness setting, formal dress was expected. Butlers helped the men with their wardrobe and other needs.

Up to 200 people could sit for dinner in the Great Hall. The meal began with a toast. Then the partners and clerks enjoyed fresh-roasted meats and new vegetables. Waiters served everyone. The upper ranks got imported goodies. They also enjoyed excellent wine and brandy.

After their meal, the Nor'westers opened the floor to dancing. They invited native women in as dance partners. Fiddles, fifes, and bagpipes played. Dances included flings and reels. The good times lasted into the early morning hours.

Balancing the Books

The days of meetings wore on. The Montreal agents brought out their account books. The wintering partners inspected them. Senior clerks explained the transactions at their trading posts. Trades that were good for the company were rewarded with a share of the profits. The clerks were encouraged to make even harder bargains in the next season.

Each partner was responsible for a trading post. It might support six families plus a few men. The total cost of each partner's business was charged to his account. All costs at the post were deducted from his furs.

Partners did not make money every year. New partners had to buy supplies for the first year in the woods. They had to purchase canoes. They had to hire men to transport trade goods. They chose the trade goods carefully. They paid for them on credit. Clerks recorded each transaction in the account books at the Counting House. It was common for a new partner to start in debt to the company.

A Bustling Summer of Trade

Fort William was a hectic place. New brigades arrived daily throughout July. Clerks opened and sorted baled goods in the warehouses. They cleaned and aired them. They made up loads to match the needs and wants of each trader's customers.

Some *hivernants* stayed only days at Fort William. Then they headed back into the northwest. They took trade goods to a drop-off point. There, the goods were picked up by another group of *hivernants*. These men travelled farther west into the Athabasca region. The *hivernants* didn't mind their short stay at Fort William. Taking goods to the fort at Lac la Pluie meant extra pay.

At Fort William, some men stayed at the fort for a week or more. They might have time for gambling or shopping at the fort's store. Philippe had to be careful not to go in debt. Paddling was the only way he had to pay off loans.

In the Equipment Shop, voyageurs could buy anything they wanted. There were guns, ammunition, knives, and tobacco. There were also bolts of cotton, beads, sewing notions, lace, blankets, and handkerchiefs. They could get their own "London Plated" beaver hat. The felt was thin. The hat was not of the best quality. However, they were very popular. Stewart and the other *hivernants* liked wearing them. Sometimes they decorated them. Ostrich feathers marked every season they spent in the *pays d'en haut*.

Bad Boys

One of the most popular items at the fort was liquor. Stories of voyageurs' drunken parties were legendary. Philippe or Stewart could tell of many times when the men got out of hand. Sometimes brawls took place between the Montreal voyageurs and the *hivernants*. Rowdy men could end up in jail for a night.

The jail was a dark and miserable place. Cells had thick solid doors. Each had only a small opening with iron bars at face-level. There were no windows in any of the walls. There was no furniture of any kind. Prisoners lay in smelly hay on the floor until they were released.

A Fort like Any Other Fort

The jailer wasn't the only hired man kept busy through the summer months. Tradesmen of all kinds produced goods. Carpenters and cabinetmakers made all the furniture at the fort. Coopers made barrels and casks for storage. In their spare time, they whittled toys for the fort's children. The tinsmith made plates and cutlery for the voyageurs. They also made candlesticks and other household items. At the armoury, guns were repaired and tested. Ammunition was sometimes made from bars of melted lead. It was poured carefully into rounded molds to create shot. The blacksmith made axes, traps, spears, canoe awls, nails, and bolts. At the fur warehouse, the pelts were sorted. The fur press compressed them into bales.

Boucher's House

Voyageurs were not welcome in the Great Hall. Instead, they went to "Boucher's House." It was a small, stone tavern just west of the fort. Jean-Marie Boucher was under contract to the North West Company. He worked for £2000 per year or one-third of the profits, whichever was higher.

At Boucher's House, the men enjoyed a cup of rum or brandy. They had to pay Boucher in "ready money." This was set in the company rules. The men had only a small amount of ready cash. Boucher often accepted the furs the voyageurs were allowed to trade. Each man could trade "two Buffalo Robes or two dressed skins" every year. Boucher then traded the furs to the company. He accepted cash, credit, or goods in return.

The voyageurs could have simple meals at Boucher's House. Even beef stew was a welcome change. The voyageurs' rations were the same at the fort as when they were on the water. Salted pork and lard were their mainstays.

The *hivernants* such as Stewart were more likely to have native or mixed-blood wives. They probably enjoyed meals of small game snared by their spouses. They might also have sugar. The making of maple sugar was a valued skill.

Native women earned credit for maple sugar at the fort. In 1816, the fort had 6231 pounds (2826 kg) of the valuable commodity in its warehouses. It was packed into *makaks*. These were large birchbark containers. Some was packed into soft wooden molds in the shape of animals. Maple syrup was kept too. It was harder to store and trade.

The Doctor Is In
The fort's doctor kept maple syrup in small amounts in the apothecary. The doctor might have used it or honey for a sore throat. The fort's doctor had a kit supplied by the company with cure-all concoctions. He would use mercury to fight disease. He also stored local roots and herbs for medicinal use.

"Bleeding" the patient was another common cure. This practice fell out of favour in time. The doctor reset limbs that were broken on the way to the fort. He wrapped them tightly with a splint. He prescribed rest for hernias. Ague was a malaria-like illness. If Philippe had it, the doctor would have treated it with a dose of arsenic. Constipation and hemorrhoids were the bane of voyageurs. The treatment was sulphur.

The War of 1812

After a week or two at the fort, the voyageurs felt rested and in good health. They got their crews back together. Then they began the work of loading the canoes for their journey home. This happened every year in the long history of the fur trade except one.

In the summer of 1812, William Mackay arrived at the fort by express canoe. He made an announcement to the partners. The Americans had declared war on Great Britain. Voyageurs were asked to volunteer for the armed forces.

The Corps of the Canadian Voyageurs was born. William McGillivray volunteered to lead them. He was a partner in the North West Company. He was also the namesake of the fort. Before long, more than 300 voyageurs had joined him in service.

The voyageurs proved to be an unruly army. According to witnesses: "They generally came on parade with a pipe in their mouths. Their rations of pork and bread were stuck on their bayonets. On parade, they talked all the time. Their officers called them to order and told them to hold their tongues. In response, one might complain, 'Ah, dear captain, let us off as quick as you can. Some of us have not yet breakfasted. And it's upwards of an hour since I had a smoke.' Nonetheless, they were loyal and willing to fight."

Commanders on both sides of the border wanted voyageurs in battle. These men were a blessing, even if they did not behave on parade. They could survive in the wild. They could follow an almost invisible trail. A voyageur could keep his men and himself from the enemy. Voyageurs fought on both sides during the war. Most based their loyalty on where their families lived or where their pay was coming from.

Smart and Strong

The Corps of Canadian Voyageurs took part in at least two major battles during the War of 1812. One was the victory over the American forces at Chrysler's Farm. (It was near present-day Kingston, Ontario.) American forces tried to conquer the British troops stationed there. However, they were outsmarted and forced to retreat.

Philippe might have been assigned to fight under Charles-Michel de Saleberry. He was stationed just south of Montreal. Word had reached the British forces that the Americans were moving north. They planned to take Montreal. The British had fewer men than the Americans. They had to come up with a brilliant battle plan. De Saleberry created a plan based on trickery instead of manpower or guns. He ordered Philippe and the others to attack the Americans. Then De Saleberry ordered a retreat. "Turn your coats inside out," he commanded. Philippe and the other men obeyed. Then they were ordered to attack again.

De Saleberry expected the tactic to confuse the enemy. He wanted the Americans to think the British forces were larger than they really were. Trumpets sounded to the east and the west, and then to the east again. The Americans were sure they were outnumbered. Were 5000 men surrounding them? The Americans retreated. The voyageurs saved Montreal from falling into American hands!

Voyageurs joined many units. More than 3000 took part in some way. The Corps of Canadian Voyageurs disbanded only six months after it began. The army released the voyageurs. After a winter with their families, the voyageurs of the North West Company were ready to work again. It was the spring of 1813. Thousands of men were still away from their homes fighting. The ones who were left were kept very busy. The fur trade suffered.

Chapter 7
End of an Era

In the decade before the War of 1812, men such as Philippe and Stewart enjoyed high earnings. It is easy to see why. The Hudson's Bay Company opened trading forts all the way to the west coast. They wanted to match the North West Company's trade methods. The North West Company would build a fort on one bank of a river. The Hudson's Bay Company built their own fort across from it. More and more men poured into the northwest.

The North West Company and the Hudson's Bay Company wanted to find new markets and beaver meadows to the west. They were not the only interested companies. Montreal was full of smaller companies that also wanted to profit. The North West Company took over some of them. Others became rivals.

The XY Company was named for the mark on its cargo bales. Its boss came from the North West Company. The venture was so successful that the directors renamed it Alexander Mackenzie & Company.

Rivalry

It was a glorious time for voyageurs such as Philippe and Stewart. They chose whom to work for and at what rate. Every company wanted the best and the fastest. They also wanted the toughest. Some voyageurs were hired on as thugs.

Competition for furs was fierce. The voyageurs weren't the only ones enjoying prosperous times. The Native peoples also benefited. A single fur of good quality was worth more and more. Hudson's Bay Company's "standard of trade" had been a brass kettle or 20 steel fish-hooks for the pelt of an adult beaver pelt. The company began to offer more for each trade. Their traders might offer a kettle plus a quarter-pound (180 grams) of tobacco or more. Some trades were more outrageous. Clerks were proud when they stole business from the competition.

Lawlessness on the Fur Trade Routes

In the middle of all this good fortune, trappers and traders became bitter rivals. To maintain business, the North West Company commonly used threats. Some of the Hudson's Bay men used violence to keep their voyageurs. They did not want them to switch companies. In one case, the Nor'Westers convinced a man from the Hudson's Bay Company post at Cumberland House to work for them. John Clarke was head of the post. His response was to kidnap several of the Nor'Westers men. The area was primed for a fight.

Clarke set out on a trading mission into the Athabasca. Several Nor'Wester canoes followed him down the river. Would they ambush him? Clarke was nervous. The Nor'Westers approached several times. Finally, they turned around and returned the way they came.

Clarke thought he could relax. However, the North West Company knew what he was up to. He and other Hudson's Bay Company men were trying to take over their territory. The Nor'Westers prepared for his arrival. They threatened their customers with violence if they traded with Clarke or his men. Nobody did. In fact, Clarke couldn't find anyone to trade with.

Clarke had been sure they would be welcomed. He hadn't brought along enough pemmican to feed his men. The Nor'Westers watched as Clarke and his men ran out of food. The Nor'Westers laughed. They did nothing to help them. They knew the voyageurs would be hungry. They would have to switch sides just to get something to eat.

Clarke tried to pretend he was still in control. He took some of his men up the Peace River. He still didn't have any food or any way to get any. Clarke left his men to search by foot for something to eat. While he was gone, the Nor'Westers swooped in. They offered the rest of Clarke's men food. Within moments, the men and all their trade goods belonged to the North West Company.

This kind of cruel behaviour spread. Brigades were ambushed. Cargo was stolen. Men were beaten. Both sides gloated over the losses of the other.

The North West Company brought in too many new partners. At the same time, they were stringing their supply line over more than 6000 kilometres. These pressures finally became too much. The partners of the North West Company began to fight amongst themselves. Then there was a dispute over charter territories and the right to trade. Officers of the Hudson's Bay Company arrested several North West Company partners at Fort William. The North West Company retaliated. All along the extended trade route, the hatred grew.

Relentless Greed

The end of the North West Company came as the exchange rate for furs increased. Beavers were now hunted all year long. The Native people's custom was to leave several beavers to repopulate the dams the following year. Even they stopped this tradition. The result was poorer quality furs and fewer adult animals. Steel traps were introduced in 1797. This led to the end of many beaver meadows.

As well, settlers were pushing beavers out of their natural habitat. Beaver meadows were drained. The exposed soil was farmed. Travel was no longer only by the waterways. Rough roads connected major cities and small towns. Journeys that once took months to travel, could now be completed in weeks. Tolls still had to be paid on private roads. In time, this became a better way of doing business. The company signed fewer long-term contracts. They hired men such as Philippe to paddle only between one point and another. Then they released them. The voyageur's way of life changed for good.

In 1821, the North West Company and the Hudson's Bay Company joined forces at last. Both companies had tried to support an impossibly long trade route. Both companies had suffered in competition.

Less than 25 years later, the 200-year reign of the beaver hat was over. In Europe, hatters used silk to make top hats instead of fur. The Canadian beaver was left in peace at last.

Epilogue

Voyageurs carried the heart of the nation for more than 200 years. They were present at many important moments in Canadian history. They were around when the country began as New France. They were still around when Canada became a country in 1867. Without them, there might not have been any cross-country trade for Europeans. That trade led to the establishment of the railroads and highways. The voyageur spirit of adventure helped define the country.

Our history preserves them in stories, pictures, and many other ways. The voyageurs have been honoured on stamps and coins. They are on the Coat of Arms for the City of Thunder Bay, Ontario. Thunder Bay is where Fort William was re-created. Groups there re-enact the travels and the history of the voyageurs. They keep the memories of the voyageurs alive.

The songs of the voyageurs still ring out along the rivers and lakes of Canada.

Glossary

allez	let's go
angus dei	a disc-shaped religious pendant
bourgeois	fur trade merchants, employers of the *coureurs de bois*
canôts du maître	large canoes about 12 metres long
canôts du nord	smaller canoes about 7 metres long
capot	hooded coat
castor gras	dirty, greasy skin of a beaver
ceintures fléchées	colourful sashes worn by voyageurs
coureurs de bois	runners of the woods (also voyageurs)
décharge	unloading a canoe for a shallow stretch of water
dégradé	run aground in shallow water
demichargé	half unload a canoe for a shallow stretch
gouvernail	steersman at the back of the canoe
governor	head of a colony
gunnel	top edge of the side of a boat
habitants	colonists/settlers of New France
hivernants	wintering voyageurs
hommes du nord	men of the north
Intendant	second in command to governor
les filles du roi	"daughters of the king"

mangeurs du lard	pork eaters
Montagnais	mountain people
patron saint	guardian/protector
pays d'en haut	country up north
perches	poles
pièce	load of goods tied together with string
portage	carrying a canoe and contents overland from one body of water to another
posé	stop
put-in	place to put canoe in river after portage
sac-à-feu	fire pouch
seigneuries	lands granted by the king to seigneurs (lords)
take-out	place to take canoe out of water before portage

Notes on places names: Hochelaga was the native name for the Ville Marie settlement which later became Montreal; Stadacona is present-day Quebec City.

Bibliography

Huck, Barbara. *Exploring the Fur Trade Routes of North America.* Winnipeg: Heartland Publications Inc., 2000.

Jennings, John and Bruce W. Hodgins and Doreen Small, editors. *The Canoe in Canadian Cultures.* Natural Heritage/Natural History Inc., 1999.

Morrison, Jean. *Superior Rendezvous-Place: Fort William in the Canadian Fur Trade.* Toronto: Natural Heritage Books, 2001.

Nute, Grace Lee. *The Voyageur.* St. Paul: Minnesota Historical Society, 1987. Reprint.

Old Fort William Staff. CD-ROM. *Northwest to the Pacific: A Fur Trade Odyssey.* Sydney: Fitzgerald Studio, 1999.

Van Kirk, Sylvia. *Many Tender Ties: Women in the Fur-Trade Society, 1670-1870.* Winnipeg: Watson & Dwyer Publishing Ltd., 1989.

Wilson, Ian, and Sally Wilson. *Wilderness Journey: Reliving the Adventures of Canada's Voyageurs.* Seattle: Gordon Soules Book Publishing, 2001.

Yates, Elizabeth. *With Pipe, Paddle and Song: A Story of the French-Canadian Voyageurs Circa 1750.* New York: E.P. Dutton & Co., Inc., 1968.

Acknowledgements

Heartfelt thanks are offered to Marty Mascarin, Shawn Patterson, and the staff at Old Fort William in Thunder Bay, Ontario. Their terrific energy and dedication to excellence in presenting living history is unequalled in North America. The author and her family will always remember the 24 hours they spent living as voyageurs with their own "Jean-Baptiste," Spencer Green, at Old Fort William.

Special thanks also to the staff at Rivers Odyssey West and the Glacier Raft Company who reminded the author just how much of an adventure racing through white water can be.

Finally, thanks to Natural Heritage Books and author Jean Morrison for the wonderful detail included in *Superior Rendezvous-Place: Fort William in the Canadian Fur Trade.*

Photo Credits

Cover: A painting by Frances Ann Hopkins entitled "Shooting the Rapids;" Glenbow Archives: pages 15 and 24.

About the Author

Marie Savage was raised in Châteauguay, Quebec, just south of Montreal near the same Kahnawake Indian Reserve mentioned in the book. She now lives in Sidney, British Columbia, with her three adventurous teenaged children. Her oldest son is a canoeing enthusiast who is training to be an outdoor adventure guide. As soon as she learns to weave, Marie will be making him a *ceintures fléchée* of his own.

Marie's work has been published in newspapers and magazines across Canada and the United States. She is a fellow of the Great Lakes Environmental Journalism Institute at Michigan State University and a CACE sustainability fellow through Western Washington University. She is the Executive Coordinator for the Urban Development Institute in Victoria, B.C. *Early Voyageurs, Junior Edition* is her third book.